River Life

Kate McGough

Contents

The Mississippi River   3

Through the Hills   4

Through the Prairies   8

Towards the Gulf of Mexico   12

Index   16

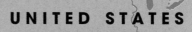

UNITED STATES

Mississippi River

The Mississippi River flows through the United States. It starts in northern Minnesota and ends in the Gulf of Mexico. Plants and animals live along the banks of the river. They live in the river, too.

The northern part of the Mississippi River flows through hills. It's cold here.

Hills

Mississippi River

Many fish live in the river. The water is clear and bright.
Rainbow trout swim in the water.

Forests line the banks of the river.

Moose live in the forests near the river. They swim in the river in summer to keep flies away. They eat underwater plants, too.

The central part of the Mississippi River winds its way through flat prairies. The river moves slower now. Tall grass grows along its banks.

Prairies

Mississippi River

Otters live in the river. They catch fish with their front paws. They can swim and eat the fish at the same time!

Muskrats live in burrows along the banks. They have flat, scaly tails. Their tails help them swim through the water.

Great blue herons live here. They wait for fish in the shallow water. They catch the fish with their sharp beaks.

The southern part of the Mississippi River flows slowly towards the Gulf of Mexico. It's warm here. The water is muddy.

Mississippi River

Gulf of Mexico

Pelicans live here. They often fish in groups. They chase fish through the water and then scoop them up in their bills.

Alligators live here, too. They crawl onto the muddy banks and lie in the warm sun.

Moss hangs from cypress trees that grow along the banks of the river. The river reaches the Gulf of Mexico.

Index

alligators 14

cypress trees 15

forests 6, 7

great blue herons 11

Gulf of Mexico 3, 12, 15

hills 4

Minnesota 3

Mississippi River 3, 4, 8, 12

moose 7

moss 15

muskrats 10

otters 9

pelicans 13

prairies 8

rainbow trout 5

United States 3